W9-BWT-805

EXPLORING JOBS IN THE GIG ECONOMY

GIG JOBS IN THE CREATIVE ARTS

by Clara MacCarald

BrightPoint Press

San Diego, CA

BrightPoint Press

an imprint of ReferencePoint Press, Inc.
Printed in the United States

For more information, contact:
BrightPoint Press
PO Box 27779
San Diego, CA 92198
www.BrightPointPress.com

LIBRARY OF CONGRESS CATALOGING-IN-PUBLICATION DATA

Names: MacCarald, Clara, 1979- author.
Title: Gig jobs in the creative arts / by Clara MacCarald.
Description: San Diego, CA: BrightPoint Press, [2023] | Includes bibliographical references and index. | Audience: Grades 10-12
Identifiers: LCCN 2022008564 (print) | LCCN 2022008565 (eBook) | ISBN 9781678203849 (hardcover) | ISBN 9781678203856 (eBook)
Subjects: LCSH: Cultural industries--Vocational guidance--Juvenile literature. | Arts--Vocational guidance--Juvenile literature. | Temporary employees--Juvenile literature. | Self-employed--Juvenile literature.
Classification: LCC HD9999.C9472 M33 2023 (print) | LCC HD9999.C9472 (eBook) | DDC 338.4/77--dc23/eng/20220304
LC record available at https://lccn.loc.gov/2022008564
LC eBook record available at https://lccn.loc.gov/2022008565

CONTENTS

AT A GLANCE

- Gig jobs in the creative arts may be individual art projects or short-term positions. Gig jobs include freelance work. They may involve crowdfunding.
- Hundreds of years ago, many books used a form of crowdfunding by using early orders to pay for printing.
- The internet gave freelancers new markets and independent artists new ways to crowdfund.
- Freelancers can be almost any kind of artist, including writers, illustrators, and musicians. Freelancers can work for magazines, websites, companies, and more.
- Artists can crowdfund on many internet platforms. They can fund a project on a website like Kickstarter or support themselves creating art on a website like Patreon.

- Gig jobs can provide artists with a lot of freedom and choices.
- Gig jobs may pay poorly. Artists doing gig work can spend much of their time working or looking for new sources of funds.
- The COVID-19 pandemic caused many artists to lose regular jobs, either in the arts or in other fields. Many of them turned to gig jobs to get by.
- The future of gig jobs in the creative arts is uncertain.

A CARTOONIST AT WORK

The camera started recording. A cartoonist named Simon Tofield sat at his desk. He moved his lamp. He set up an ink drawing. It was a Christmas scene. Tofield's cartoon character Simon was opening presents. Simon's cat was knocking over the Christmas tree. Tofield began adding lines to the picture.

Some artists prefer to draw exclusively by hand, while others use digital technology like tablets. Many artists use a combination of both.

The characters were from the cartoon Simon's Cat. Tofield posted his first Simon's Cat video in 2008. He has written books and made comics for the series. He also

Some artists are hired to work on a specific project. Others make their own art and sell it themselves.

posts videos to internet **platforms** such as YouTube. Artists like him can earn income from creating content for the internet. Making money this way is a part of the **gig** economy in the creative arts.

When Tofield is happy with the drawing, he uploads it to a computer. He starts adding color to the picture using a special pen. The movements of the pen on a pad make color appear on the screen. Red sweeps over the walls. Simon's sweater turns red and green. The ornaments become colorful.

Finally, the picture is finished. The video is not. Before ending up online, the video will need to be put together and music added. The completed video will join many others on the Simon's Cat YouTube channel.

CREATIVE GIGS

Gig jobs aren't regular jobs with a steady income. Gig workers may be freelancers who do work for several different clients. They may be independent workers who get money for each project. The gig economy is huge and growing. In 2021, about a third of workers in the United States did some kind of gig work.

Gig workers in the creative arts are not limited to one kind of art. Gig workers include writers, illustrators, musicians, and filmmakers. They can be artists who use internet platforms to **crowdfund** one

Freelance photographers often have a specialty. This may be something like weddings or other special events.

project at a time. Or they can be artists who make money by creating content to post online.

CHAPTER ONE

THE HISTORY OF GIG JOBS IN THE CREATIVE ARTS

The roots of gig jobs in the creative arts go back a long way. People were doing things similar to modern crowdfunding to support the creation of art hundreds of years ago. Writers and artists have long contributed stories and illustrations to magazines.

The word gig was first used by jazz musicians. Musicians are often hired for one performance at a time.

The internet created many new opportunities for artists. New online platforms gave independent artists cheap ways to reach more fans. Crowdfunding websites gave creators new sources of support.

MAGAZINES TO WEBSITES

Magazines have been a very important market for gig workers. Stories, illustrations, and photos in a magazine often come from freelancers. Magazines first appeared in the late 1600s. Starting in the 1800s, cheap magazines became popular. Magazines hired authors to write stories. They also ran comics and illustrations. Magazines with photos became popular in the mid-1900s.

In the 1990s, print magazines gained a new competitor: online magazines. Printing a physical magazine requires a lot of money. The publisher must pay for

Both print and online magazines often use freelance writers and photographers.

paper. Publishers must pay to mail the magazine out to **subscribers**. Magazines that are only online don't have those costs. Yet online magazines can reach a vast number of readers. The first major online magazine was *Salon*. It started in 1995. As of 2021, *Salon* had around 10 million visitors a month.

The internet led to many new markets for freelancers. Some websites didn't call themselves magazines but offered similar content. Many print magazines decided to create their own websites. Like magazines, websites need fresh content.

A HISTORY OF CROWDFUNDING

Freelancers create content for clients. Artists also produce independent projects. One way to fund a project is with crowdfunding. Before the internet, people didn't use the word *crowdfunding*. However, many people did something similar. They sought to fund projects with money from a

Early books were expensive to publish. Printers had to put each letter into a machine called a printing press.

large group of people. In the 1600s, some publishers took orders from readers before they printed a book. The money covered the printing costs. The supporters got the book when it was finished.

Musicians in the 1700s who didn't have jobs needed rich supporters. Supporters could give the musicians funds. Some provided an allowance. In 1783, Wolfgang Amadeus Mozart had an idea. He wanted to play three shows at a hall in Vienna, Austria. But he needed to finance the series. The way he looked for funds looked a lot like modern crowdfunding. He sent letters to several rich people asking for money. In return, he promised to give them copies of his printed music. It took more than two years for Mozart to have enough money for his shows.

For a long time, crowdfunding happened through letters and newspaper articles.

Mozart was an Austrian composer in the late 1700s. He wrote hundreds of pieces of music.

But the internet changed everything. Artists could quickly and cheaply reach a large group of possible backers. In 1996, the British rock band Marillion wanted to tour North America. But they needed money. An online campaign raised $60,000 from fans to make it happen.

In 2001, Brian Camelio started a website called ArtistShare. ArtistShare was the first online platform for crowdfunding. "I was starting to worry about the future of music," Camelio explained.[1] He worried about how musicians were getting money for their craft. He thought it would help if fans could connect with artists in a personal way.

The idea was that fans supported an artist's projects through ArtistShare. The artist offered special deals in exchange. Supporters could watch videos of the artist creating things. Or they might get a free

A WHALE OF AN EMOJI

In 2009, Fred Benenson created one of the earliest Kickstarter campaigns. Benenson proposed to turn Herman Melville's *Moby Dick* into a book written entirely with emojis. After a month, Benenson had the $3,676 he'd asked for. He paid people to help with the task. In 2010, he finished. Supporters received the published book. Others could buy themselves a copy.

album before the public could buy it. Other crowdfunding platforms soon followed.

Starting in 2007, the world economy suffered a downturn. It was called the Great Recession. Millions of people lost money and jobs. Funding for the arts was cut. Many artists turned to the internet. In 2008, the major crowdfunding site IndieGoGo came online. The next year it was joined by the website Kickstarter. Crowdfunding was on the rise.

CONTENT CREATION ONLINE

There was also an increase in opportunities to share creative content online. One method was by starting a **blog**. Student Justin Hall started what is believed to be the original blog in 1994. At the time, it wasn't called a blog. Hall called it his homepage instead. The word *weblog* was created in 1997. *Weblog* was shortened to *blog* two years later.

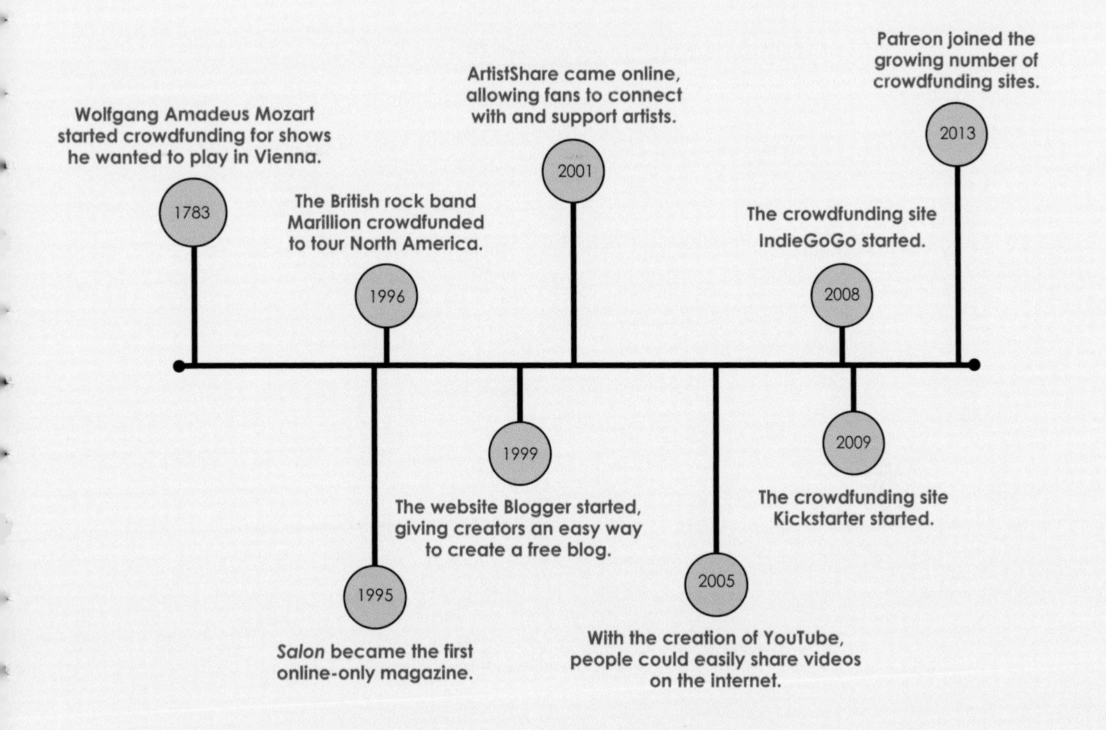

Early forms of gig work and crowdfunding have been around for hundreds of years. The internet helped artists connect with new audiences.

At first, Hall just linked to different websites. Over time he created his own content. "The early Web did not appear to be very interesting," Hall said, to explain why he shared his own writing and pictures.[2] The website received a lot of attention. The blog helped him land regular jobs as well as freelance work writing about gaming.

Some people followed Hall's example. But the internet was a different place back then. Not everyone could make a website. Hall had a chance to do so only because he was a student at a college with internet access. In a few years things changed. More people got online. The popular website Blogger started in 1999. Creating a blog on Blogger was free and easy. Soon other blogging platforms were created.

There are many websites that allow people to create blogs. Wix, Blogger, and WordPress are popular sites.

Content creators started looking to make money off their blogs. Businesses took notice of how popular blogs were becoming. There was a huge marketing opportunity. Other websites made money by showing ads. In 2003, Google created AdSense. AdSense would show ads on a blog based on the blog's content. Bloggers earned money from the ads.

Other platforms appeared that let artists share creative content. YouTube started in 2005. The site allowed users to share videos. Artists could earn income from ad money. And YouTube videos could lead to offers for other gigs.

In 2013, Patreon started. The platform helped creators crowdfund using their online content. Unlike other crowdfunding sites, Patreon let fans support artists with regular payments rather than giving money just once. People make monthly payments to view or listen to art. Over time, gig jobs in the creative arts have continued to grow.

JACK CONTE AND PATREON

Jack Conte began as a musician. He played in a band called Pomplamoose. Pomplamoose posted music to YouTube in the late 2000s. It also sold products and songs. In the early 2010s, the band started relying on ad money. In 2012, Conte spent thousands of dollars on a music video. He even made a fake spaceship. But he realized if a million people saw the video, he would only make around $160. The experience was part of what inspired him to help create Patreon.

CHAPTER TWO

WORKING A GIG JOB IN THE CREATIVE ARTS

There are plenty of opportunities for people to find gig jobs in the creative arts. Businesses need art for products and marketing. Many online platforms exist to connect artists with fans willing to pay to support art.

Many businesses work with artists to design logos or marketing materials for products.

Some artists have a regular job and work gig jobs on the side. An artist doesn't have to stay with one kind of gig job, either. An artist may create online content, crowdfund, and sell art to people at the same time.

Writers can choose to release their own pieces on personal websites or blogs, or they can work with publications like magazines.

FREELANCE JOBS

Any kind of artist can look for freelance jobs. All it requires is a skill and a client who needs that skill. A freelancer can be a writer, a visual artist, a filmmaker, or something else. Over time, freelancers build connections with different clients. These connections help them find work in the future.

Some freelancers write stories or articles for newspapers and magazines. Writers can also find gig jobs producing content for blogs and websites. The writer might have to spend time studying a topic before writing.

Many kinds of businesses use freelance illustrators. A business may want art for its ads. Illustrators can create characters for books, films, or video games. Magazines and websites use work from illustrators.

A photographer can also take jobs doing many different things. A company might need pictures of its products for marketing. A publisher might need photos for a book. Some freelance photographers use smartphone cameras. But for professional

A GIG ARTIST

Like many artists, watercolor artist Maria Raczynska has found multiple ways to support her art online. She began with a YouTube channel. She shared videos of herself showing viewers how to paint. Later she joined Patreon, offering videos to subscribers. Raczynska has an Etsy page too. On her YouTube channel she sells products decorated with her art. Her personal website sells finished pieces and allows people to hire her for specific projects.

photos, a photographer may need a high-quality camera. A personal **studio** is a good place to take shots of people or objects. Other shoots may require photographers to travel.

Many companies look for filmmakers. A freelance filmmaker might produce videos for a company's website or YouTube channel. A video might be an ad for a product. Freelancers can also take gigs working on films or television shows. Filmmakers may work with a smartphone and laptop. Some projects may require professional gear.

Artists can use social media to promote their work and to gain an audience. This also allows them to make money without depending on traditional establishments like art galleries.

To get jobs, freelancers often show some of their work online. New clients can check out a creator's blog or website. Freelancers can also post work to social media platforms such as Instagram. While on the job, freelancers often work closely with the client to make sure the project follows the client's vision.

CROWDFUNDING CAMPAIGNS

Many different platforms for crowdfunding exist. The platforms often charge artists a fee to use the website. They may also charge a fee every time a person gives the creator money. Artists can fund almost any sort of project through these platforms. They can run a campaign to publish a book or comic. They can seek funding to make a film or play. Other art forms people crowdfund include music, podcasts, photography, and illustration.

Artists have to make people want to fund their work. They must explain the project in a catchy way. Often the explanation is in writing. Artists can also use a video or pictures. In 2014, Brian Foo ran a campaign to publish a book. Foo had advice for people putting a campaign video together. He said, "Tell a story, show that you're a normal person." He recommended that people "be as genuine as possible."[3]

The artist has to decide on rewards and prizes to give to people who provide funds.

Even small films can cost thousands of dollars to make. Crowdfunding is one strategy filmmakers can use to raise money.

Some rewards are products. Artists can create special stickers, mugs, or pieces of art. The products can be digital, such as videos or music files. Artists might promise to produce these things after the campaign is over. Other rewards are experiences.

A fan might get the chance to hang out with the artist in person or online.

CREATING CONTENT

Many artists post videos to YouTube to earn money. Some money comes from ads. But to benefit from ads, a creator needs a certain number of views and subscribers. Some artists find sponsors. A sponsor is usually a company that provides funds to support the creator's content. The creator advertises the company's products. For example, artists might receive free pens from an art company that sponsors their channel. They can post videos showing themselves drawing with the pens.

A blogger can also run ads and have sponsors. Some blogs have something called affiliate links. Affiliate links take a reader to an online store. If the reader buys something there, the online store pays some

ETSY

Etsy is an online market for many handmade goods. Sellers make an account and open their own shop on the site. On their shop's page they list each product they have for sale. High quality pictures of the products help to sell them. When a buyer makes a purchase, the seller packages and ships the order. Artists can sell objects such as jewelry. Artists can also sell computer files of art.

of the money to the blog owner. Artists can sell their own products on blogs or a platform like YouTube. Fans may pay the artist to create a piece of art just for them. Artists can also sell products on sites such as Etsy.

Some platforms allow artists greater control over how their content makes money. Patreon is a popular example. Almost any kind of content can go on Patreon. Examples include writing, illustrations, sound recordings, and music. Fans subscribe to an artist's Patreon page. One digital artist who uses Patreon says,

There are different ways creators can reward people who fund them. Videos are one example.

"I think Patreon is a place that you need to prove yourself."[4] He suggested artists need fans to feel they are getting enough value for their money.

Fans can pay more for more content or rewards. For example, people who pay one dollar a month might get to see illustrations online. For five dollars a month, they might be able to see the illustrations as well as get stickers in the mail. For ten, they might also get to watch art classes. Or the creator could mention supporters during a video or podcast as a reward.

According to Patreon, early access to content, merchandise, and exclusive content are some of the most popular rewards for supporters.

CHAPTER THREE

PROS AND CONS OF GIG JOBS IN THE CREATIVE ARTS

Gig jobs can provide a lot of opportunities. They allow artists to do what they love while earning money. But gig jobs also come with many challenges. Gig workers must weigh the benefits and drawbacks.

The gig economy can help artists follow their passions without needing a traditional full-time job.

PROS OF GIG WORK

Gig workers can have a lot of control over their jobs. They might be able to work wherever they want. Sometimes that means working from home. Sometimes that means choosing to work somewhere else.

Gig workers can often work from anywhere. Many choose to travel or take jobs far away from where they live.

Freelance writer Jason Brick said, "I took my family to Malaysia for 13 months, and half my clients didn't notice I'd left."[5]

In a regular job, workers usually have a set schedule and earn a set amount of pay. Gig workers often have more control of their work. They can create their own schedule.

They have the freedom to take a day off. Sometimes they set their own fees. They can choose to work more to earn more. Some gig workers make a good amount of money. Top creators can make thousands of dollars a month on Patreon. Other workers might make just enough to get by or to add to another source of income.

Gig workers do a lot of different projects. If one job is unpleasant, the artist can look forward to the next one. Freelancers often have opportunities to work with many interesting people on many interesting projects. They can take on different jobs to learn different skills. For example, a writer could work on social media posts for one gig. She may write formal papers for another.

When freelancers start out, they can't pick and choose gigs as easily. With success comes greater power. A freelancer who is doing well can decide who to work for or what to work on.

CONS OF GIG WORK

An artist might take on too many jobs by accident. Perhaps he thought he could get all the work done on time. Maybe some jobs took more hours of effort than

Some of the top creators on Patreon make podcasts. Other popular categories include video creators, gamers, and musicians.

he expected. Or something could have happened in the artist's personal life. Even one job could require more hours of work than the artist had scheduled. When gig workers fall behind, they might have to work through the holidays or all night to catch up. Some artists almost never take a break, even on vacation.

When gig workers set their own fees, they may charge too little for the work they end up doing. Or an artist may promise too many rewards during a crowdfunding campaign. Artists may end up losing money on a project.

The pay for some gigs can be very low too. For example, a YouTube video can get millions of views but earn less than a dollar. And videos that break YouTube's rules can be stripped of ad money. One rule is that artists can't play a song that is owned by someone else on their videos. If an artist posts a video that has music, they can lose ad money.

Gig workers don't get many of the benefits of a regular job. A freelance writer won't get paid sick days or vacations, for example. No matter how hard artists

FAMOUS YOUTUBE MUSICIANS

A small number of YouTube musicians make it big. Justin Bieber started out by posting songs he recorded at home. Later he signed with a record company and sold millions of albums. Tori Kelly had some experiences on television that went nowhere. But her YouTube content led to a career. She ended up winning two Grammy awards as of 2021. Ed Sheeran was playing live shows before, but his work on YouTube made him a superstar. Billions of people have viewed his YouTube videos.

work, some months they will earn less and some months they will earn more. The change in income can be difficult to plan for. Everyone has living expenses. They must pay for a place to live, food to eat, and other important things. Gig workers must save money for times when they have fewer jobs. To get by, some gig workers end up taking jobs they don't like in order to make more money.

Gig workers spend a lot of time selling themselves. Many freelance artists are always applying to new clients, even in the middle of a job. They need to look online,

Gig workers get paid only when they are actively working for customers. This can be very stressful.

send emails to people, and ask friends for leads. An artist looking to crowdfund spends a lot of time and work getting people interested in the project. This time is unpaid.

PROS AND CONS OF CROWDFUNDING

Using a crowdfunding platform can be a cheap way to start getting income. Many different crowdfunding platforms exist. Artists have lots of choice. Artists can try the one that seems best for meeting their goals. Different websites can charge different fees. Or platforms can collect fees in different ways.

Crowdfunding can lead to other kinds of work. It can give artists a way to catch the attention of a vast number of people who might be interested in their art. A crowdfunding gig can catch the attention of a business that needs artists. The artist might get hired. A recording company might sign a musician making internet content. A popular blog might lead to a book deal with a publisher.

Artists running a campaign must carefully consider how much money to ask for. Ludenso is a company that had success

PLATFORM FEES

Creators have many ways to make money on platforms. But platforms also need to make money. To do this, there are often fees. Kickstarter charges 5 percent of the total funds from a successful campaign. The site also takes some money from each payment. Patreon takes money from each payment too. The platform has fee levels that start at 5 percent.

on a Kickstarter campaign. The campaign funded goggles that showed films to the people wearing them. The team at Ludenso gave advice to other people crowdfunding a single project. They wrote, "You should be absolutely sure that you can complete your project with the amount funded."[6] Otherwise, once the campaign is over, the artist could struggle to find more money to meet his or her goal.

Not every project gets the funds it needs. However, that can be a good thing. If a piece of art doesn't have buyers, the artist may need to improve his or her idea.

Hearing from the public can help the artist decide what to change. The experience may even give the artist ideas for a new project.

PLATFORM BANS

Sometimes platforms ban users. Both Patreon and YouTube have been among those trying to remove people who encourage hate or share false information. But this has had mixed success. Some users have complained about creators who break the rules without getting banned. Other users have complained about the practice. For example, a popular writer and podcaster named Sam Harris left Patreon to protest bans.

CHAPTER FOUR

THE FUTURE OF GIG JOBS IN THE CREATIVE ARTS

After 2008, gig jobs in the creative arts continued to grow. Opportunities spread across the internet. The gig economy steadily got bigger. Many artists began to depend on it. Then, in 2020, the world changed. And so did the creative gig economy.

Many people lost their jobs in the COVID-19 pandemic. Some of them turned to gig work.

CREATIVE SHUTDOWN

On March 11, 2020, the World Health Organization announced that an illness called COVID-19 had become a **pandemic**. Governments told people to stay home as much as possible. This would slow the spread of the disease. Millions of people lost or left jobs. People weren't spending as much money outside the home. Some artists had their gig jobs paused or ended. People stopped holding many events. Companies also hesitated to spend money

THE APPEAL OF SUBSTACK

Substack is a paid newsletter platform that was founded in 2017. Writers and other creators charge subscribers a monthly fee. In return, the subscribers get newsletters and other content. Substack has started paying writers, journalists, and even comic book writers to join the site. Creators like this model because they have creative freedom. During the early part of the COVID-19 pandemic, large events like sports were paused. Many sports journalists lost work. Some turned to Substack to pay their bills.

on ads. With fewer ads, creators on platforms like YouTube lost earnings.

Many independent artists who lost income turned to crowdfunding platforms. Tens of thousands of creators joined sites like Patreon. Many writers started using the platform Substack, which allowed them to make money from newsletters. The newsletters can include anything the person wants to write about. They range from made-up stories to serious reporting. Some people who once had regular jobs started looking for freelance gigs.

When COVID-19 hit, musicians couldn't make money from live shows anymore. They had to find new ways to earn money and connect with fans.

Like many, an artist named Annie had been posting art on the side already. She said, "When I lost my job I turned to my followers for help, opened up my Ko-fi account, and within the first day it was unbelievable."[7] Many fans and friends wanted to help support her through her difficult time.

People avoided crowds because of the pandemic. Live music shows and theater suffered. Many musicians were stuck at home instead of being able to tour. Some turned to platforms that let them livestream their music to fans.

A major platform for streaming videos live was Twitch. When Twitch started, it was mostly people streaming themselves playing video games. But people began sharing almost any kind of content on the website.

Other platforms musicians could use to stream included Bandsintown and TikTok.

FIGHTING OVER CREATORS

In 2021, platforms such as Instagram and Twitter were trying to make themselves more appealing to gig workers. One way was by offering more methods for earning money, such as tips and subscription fees. Patreon made plans to improve its services and invite all sorts of creators onto the platform, even famous people.

The company Snap owns Snapchat. Snapchat is a messaging app. Users can share videos as well as pictures. In 2021,

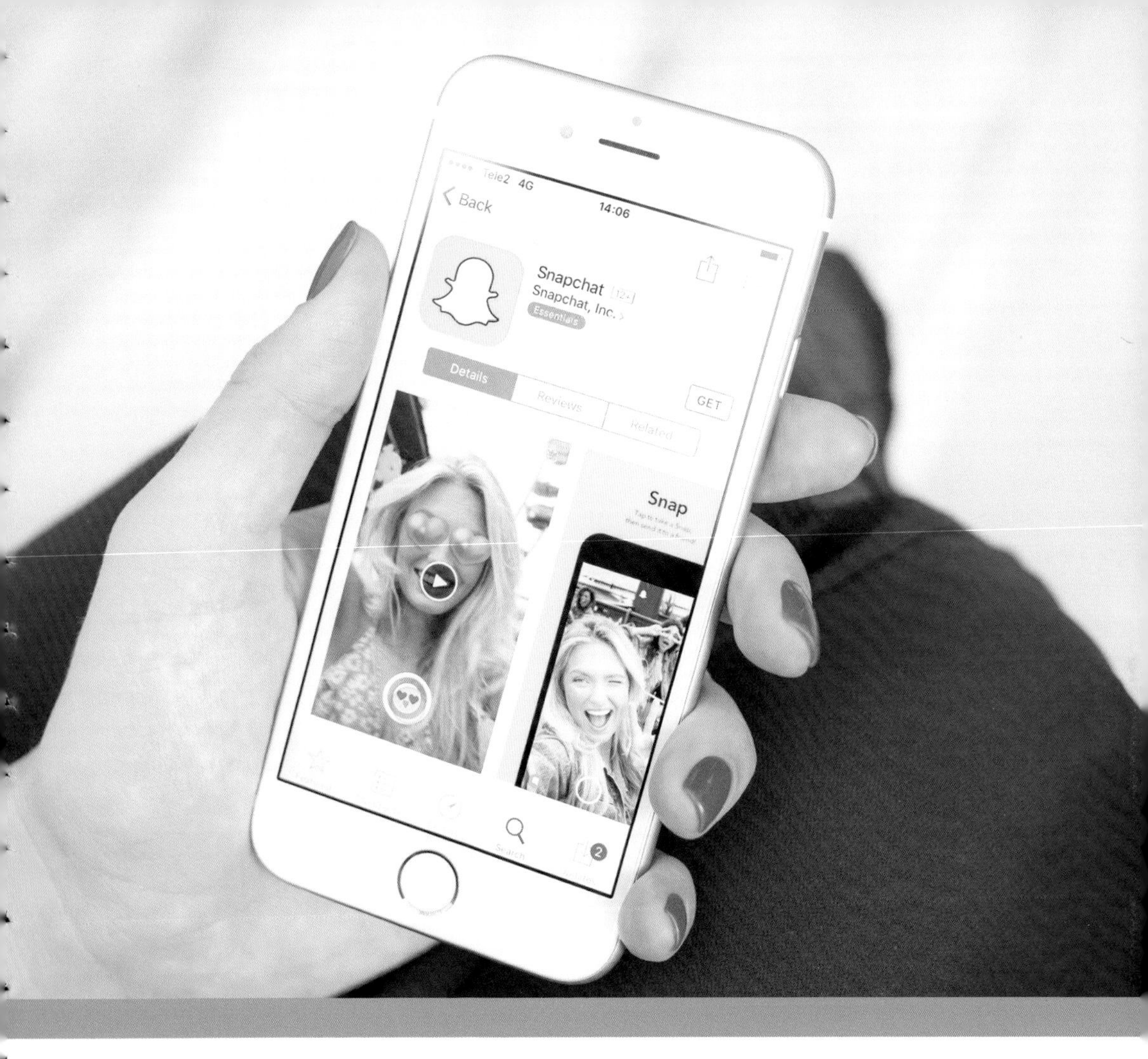

Snapchat is a messaging app that launched in 2011.

Snap started holding contests to inspire more original content from their users. Each contest had a challenge. These challenges required videos with certain features.

Snap gave money as prizes to the creators who did the best job.

YouTube also made changes to encourage creators. The company had a feature that let users easily create and post very short videos. YouTube called them Shorts. The videos were modeled after similar videos on rival platforms like TikTok and Snapchat. At first the feature was available in only some parts of the world. In 2021, YouTube brought the feature to the United States.

In August 2021, YouTube executive Robert Kyncl announced a new fund.

The Shorts Fund gave prize money to people making the most popular Shorts. YouTube based this on how many viewers watched or interacted with the video. "With the launch of the Shorts Fund," Kyncl said, "creators and artists now have 10 ways

FUNDING BLACK CREATORS

YouTube created the #YouTubeBlack Voices Fund in 2020. The company made the move after the rise of the Black Lives Matter movement. People pointed out that YouTube had a problem with hate speech spreading on its platform. As one attempt to improve the situation, the $100 million fund supported Black creators as well as the content they made. People who received money from the fund had opportunities to take courses to gain business and art skills.

to make money and build a business on YouTube."[8] Other ways to make money included the things a creator could sell while streaming. Fans could buy the chance to post special messages that would stand out in the chat. They could also buy digital stickers to add to messages.

A FUTURE AFTER COVID-19

During the pandemic, people who were lucky enough to keep regular jobs often couldn't work at the office. They worked from home to stop the spread of COVID-19. With that experience, more people became open to the idea of gig

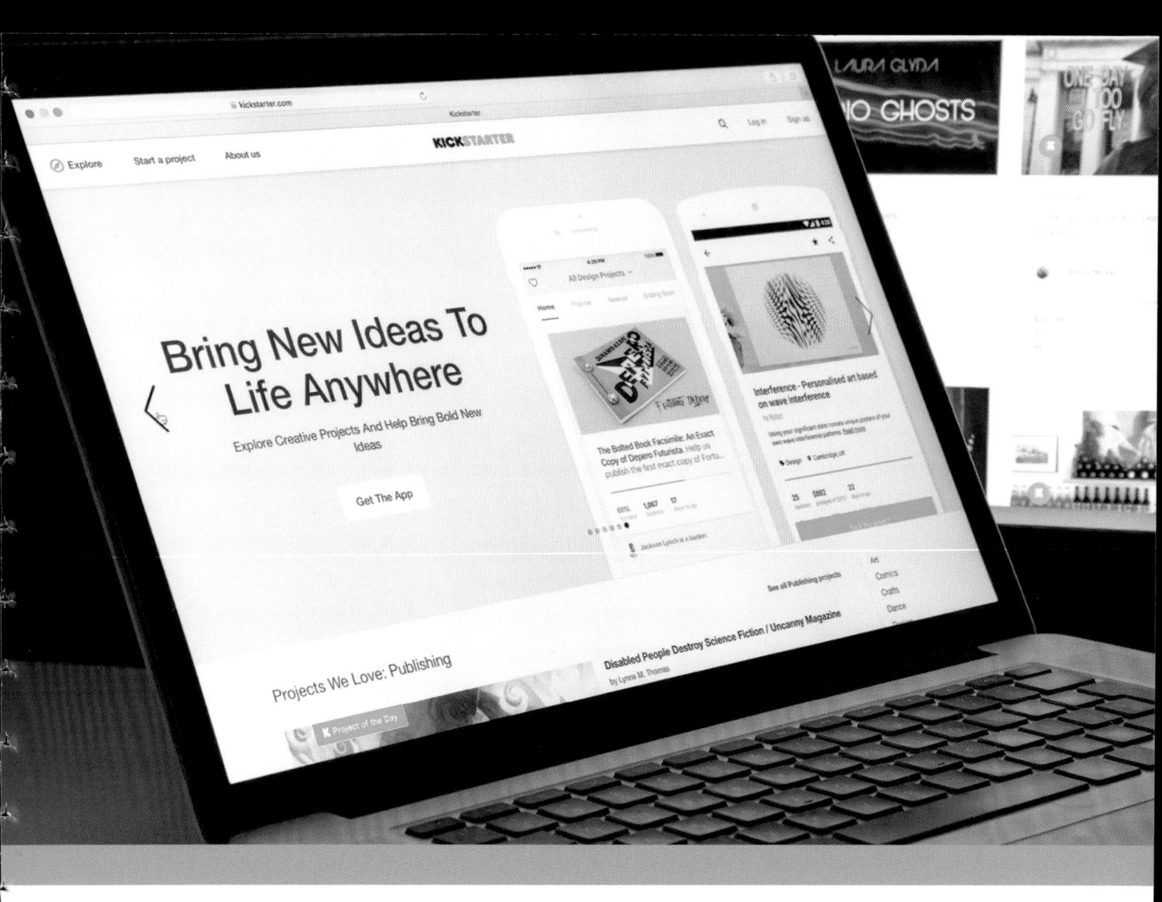

As of 2021, Kickstarter had helped creators raise more than $6.2 billion for projects.

work. Many people who started freelancing during the pandemic began to see it as an ongoing career.

The pandemic had huge effects on the economy. Some of the changes hurt gig work. Many companies spent less money on freelancers. With a loss of jobs and income, some people were less likely to give money to crowdfunded projects. Kickstarter noted a slowdown in 2020. The site had 35 percent fewer campaigns than the year before. Kickstarter looked at ways to encourage more campaigns. It started a program to celebrate creators who tried very small projects they could finish from home.

At the same time, Kickstarter also moved to shut down campaigns that included false information about COVID-19. Kickstarter wasn't the only platform cracking down

There are many benefits and drawbacks to gig work in the creative arts.

on creators. In 2021, Indiegogo created a group to look closely at crowdfunding campaigns. The group could shut down campaigns with projects that were very unlikely to succeed even with funds.

The group could also ban users who didn't honor their promises.

The future of gig jobs in the creative arts is unclear. Artists may flock to new platforms. Old platforms may continue to change to try to appeal to creators. Businesses may provide new opportunities for freelance artists. But however it ends up changing, the creative gig economy is likely here to stay.

There are many ways to work in the gig economy. Artists and creators will have to decide whether it is the best choice for them.

GLOSSARY

blog

a website meant for posting regular writings

crowdfund

to raise money by getting small amounts from many people

gig

a short-term job or project

pandemic

an illness occurring all over the world

platforms

online programs or services that allow people to interact with each other

studio

a place or room where an artist works

subscribers

people who pay money on a regular basis for a product

SOURCE NOTES

CHAPTER ONE: THE HISTORY OF GIG JOBS IN THE CREATIVE ARTS

1. Quoted in "Can You Spare a Quarter? Crowdfunding Sites Turn Fans into Patrons of the Arts," *Knowledge @ Wharton*, December 8, 2010. https://knowledge.wharton.upenn.edu.

2. Quoted in Lene Bech Sillesen, "Is This the Web's First Blog?" *Columbia Journalism Review*, November 5, 2015. https://archives.cjr.org.

CHAPTER TWO: WORKING A GIG JOB IN THE CREATIVE ARTS

3. Quoted in Natalie Ung, "One Question, Six Creators: What Makes a Good Project Page?" *Kickstarter*, May 6, 2014. www.kickstarter.com.

4. Quoted in Melody Nieves, "How Artists Make a Living with Patreon," *Evato Tuts+*, October 22, 2020. https://design.tutsplus.com.

CHAPTER THREE: PROS AND CONS OF GIG JOBS IN THE CREATIVE ARTS

5. Jason Brick, "Top 8 Benefits of Freelance Writing," *TCK Publishing*, n.d. www.tckpublishing.com.

6. Quoted in "How to Launch a Successful Kickstarter Campaign," *Innovate@BU*, n.d. www.bu.edu/innovate.

CHAPTER FOUR: THE FUTURE OF GIG JOBS IN THE CREATIVE ARTS

7. Quoted in Shubham Agarwal, "Patreon and Ko-fi Become Full-Time Gigs as Creators Lose Their Jobs," *Digital Trends*, April 25, 2020. www.digitaltrends.com.

8. Robert Kyncl, "10 Ways to Monetize on YouTube," *YouTube Official Blog*, August 3, 2021. https://blog.youtube.

FOR FURTHER RESEARCH

BOOKS

A. W. Buckey, *Gig Jobs in Social Media*. San Diego, CA: BrightPoint Press, 2023.

Bridey Heing, *The Gig Economy*. New York: Greenhaven Publishing, 2021.

Anna Leigh, *Write and Record Your Own Songs*. Minneapolis, MN: Lerner Publications, 2018.

INTERNET SOURCES

Andrew R. Chow, "Digital Art Boom," *Time for Kids*, October 15, 2021. www.timeforkids.com.

Andrew Hirschfeld, "Can Patreon and Twitch Drive the New Gig Economy?" *Ozy*, September 2020. www.ozy.com.

Abby Young-Powell, "What I Wish I Had Known About Freelancing in the Arts," *Guardian*, February 1, 2018. www.theguardian.com.

WEBSITES

Art & Design Inspiration

https://artanddesigninspiration.com

Art & Design Inspiration offers tips, articles, and inspiration for artists.

Art Station Magazine

https://magazine.artstation.com

Art Station Magazine includes news about the art industry, inspiration for artists, and resources to improve art skills.

National Gallery of Art

www.nga.gov

The National Gallery of Art in Washington, DC, is a museum that has more than 150,000 pieces of art.

INDEX

IMAGE CREDITS

Cover: © Raw Pixel/Shutterstock Images
5: © Jacob Lund/Shutterstock Images
7: © David Ferencik/Shutterstock Images
8: © Ross Helen/Shutterstock Images
11: © Vipubadee/Shutterstock Images
13: © Dragon Images/Shutterstock Images
15: © Niloo/Shutterstock Images
17: © Everett Collection/Shutterstock Images
19: © Anibal Trejo/Shutterstock Images
23: © Red Line Editorial
25: © Dean Drobot/Shutterstock Images
29: © Red Pixel Pl./Shutterstock Images
30: © Raw Pixel/Shutterstock Images
34: © Golubovy/Shutterstock Images
37: © Abdullah Killinc/iStockphoto
41: © Sofikos S./Shutterstock Images
43: © Light Field Studios/Shutterstock Images
45: © Ross Helen/Shutterstock Images
46: © Bell Ka Pang/Shutterstock Images
49: © Kmpzzz/Shutterstock Images
53: © Syda Productions/Shutterstock Images
59: © Eugenio Marongiu/Shutterstock Images
62: © GBJ Stock/Shutterstock Images
65: © Kaspars Grinvalds/Shutterstock Images
69: © Casimiro PT/Shutterstock Images
71: © Free Pik 2/Shutterstock Images
73: © Eng. Bilal Izaddin/Shutterstock Images

ABOUT THE AUTHOR

Clara MacCarald is a freelance writer with a master's degree in ecology and natural resources. She lives with her family in an off-grid house nestled in the forests of central New York. When not parenting her daughter, she spends her time writing nonfiction books for kids.